Copyright Page

I0493286

Contents

About the Author

Dr. Billy R. Williams, the writer of this book, has spent the last 14 years and 100s of thousands of dollars on real world, trial-and-error-based business building, to bring you proven marketing campaigns that will make your business a magnet for inbound prospects when you implement the marketing campaigns, technology, and conversations explained in this book.

Forever the consummate over-achiever, he is the president of the Williams Family Agency Investment Group Inc., a group of 40+ general insurance agencies around the country that currently produce more than $600 Million in new and renewal business annually.

He is also the founder and president of Inspire a Nation Business Mentoring Services, a coaching and mentoring company that specializes in helping small business that are operating on a limited marketing budget. Inspire a Nation Business Mentoring programs help 100s of small business owners from a variety of industry types to implement marketing, sales, service processes, and tools that help to grow their businesses, often on a shoestring budget.

A word from the author

The formula for Business Luck is: Opportunity + Preparation + Time Management = Business Luck.

By applying the information presented in this book you will create more total business opportunities because of the timing and preparation of your marketing and advertising campaigns.

My intent is to write this book in such a way that it becomes a very important part of your business reference library. I do have a couple of requests of you: if this book adds value to your business I need you to write a positive review about the book. You can write your positive review on whatever site you used to purchase this book such as Amazon, Google Books, or LuLu, or you can email your positive review to helpdesk@inspireanation.org.

The next request is that you share this book with one or two of your business associates. The easiest way to share the book is to provide the link that you used to purchase the book, however, you can also have them text their email address to 682-200-1808 or direct them to my company website at www.inspireanation.org.

You can stay up to date on all of our training and mentoring programs by downloading our mobile app https://inspireanationmentoring.appsme.com. Now the top business mentors are on your smart phone.

Throughout this book I will share with you the exact campaigns, inbound Calls-to-Action, and inbound Call-to-Action wording we use at Inspire a Nation Business Mentoring and my partner companies to drive 100s of inbound prospects on a daily basis to our solutions. So buckle up and experience the ride!

Introduction

Let's be honest, we all hate cold call prospecting!

We tolerate warm call prospecting, but we love when a prospect calls, emails, or walks in our office and wants to talk to us about our product or service.

Effective Inbound Marketing is a direct result of consistent marketing and advertising that identifies a problem and/or emotional trigger and provides easy to implement Calls-to-Action. Let me stress this again: you can't have an effective inbound marketing culture in your business without effective and consistent marketing and advertising! You can only turn water into wine if you have water to begin with, and your phones are not going to ring if you don't have any marketing or advertising happening in your business.

Many small businesses don't have a marketing and advertising list of prospects. You have several options to generate a prospect list:

1. Use an existing list of current and former customers,

2. Use Facebook and Google Ads to reach a target audience,

3. Use the Every Door Direct Mail option from the US Postal service (https://www.usps.com/business/every-door-direct-mail.htm) to mail your marketing and advertising materials to specific carrier routes in a selected city,

4. Collect business cards and use the information on the cards to create a marketing list,

5. Use social networking contacts. If you don't have any social networking contacts, start connecting today!

6. Another old-school option is to use the yellow pages and white pages to start a contact list you can mail. This usually works best for business to business sales. You can mail the business list or you can also send an automated call to businesses and use a survey or a "press 1 now for more information" call to action to generate inbound activity. Business phone numbers generally do not fall under the Do Not Call rules (Check the federal guidelines from the FCC, FTC, and State before sending any type of auto dialer call to a prospect)

7. Finally, if you do have some funds available, you can purchase prospecting lists from vendors like InfoUsa or MelissaData. Often they give you the option to purchase email lists as well as lists you can mail.

The main issue I want this book to solve for you is where to find a quick-reference of marketing campaigns that: match your marketing personality, use great Calls-to-Action, and utilize a variety of marketing and advertising campaigns that tap into the emotional and situational triggers of your target prospects. With all that being said, let's dig deeper into inbound marketing.

Marketing and Advertising vs Prospecting Campaigns

Marketing and Advertising (Drives Inbound Prospects) - The prospect is expected to contact you because of marketing materials that they see or are exposed to. Examples include: emails, mailings, video, radio, articles, television, etc.

Prospecting (Outbound) – You contact the prospect because of information you have about the prospect. Examples include: an upcoming birthday contact, email or phone call because of an expiring service, they have a new baby, they recently moved, or they requested information, etc.

What makes inbound marketing so powerful is that you are eliminating or at least minimizing the one area of prospecting that most people hate . . . the dreaded cold call! In addition, it is psychologically easier to talk to someone that you know already has an interest in your product or service. Finally, your close ratio skyrockets when marketing is inbound based versus outbound.

Just think of how many more calls in a day you would be willing to make if you were calling people that: requested information about your product or service, voluntarily provided their contact information, and expected a call or outreach from you.

Making your business a magnet for inbound prospects will accomplish this while saving you thousands of dollars on marketing and advertising, and without the burn out that comes with cold calling.

You can never eliminate prospect follow-up (nor should you ever want to!) but I will show you how to drive inbound calls that will make prospect follow-up a pleasure instead of a chore.

A Spider's Web

Let's use the analogy of a spider to help you understand how inbound marketing should work in your business.

A spider generally does not have good eyesight and can't chase its prey to catch and feed off of it;

Spiders build their webs where they feel they are most likely to catch a good supply of food;

Their webs have lots of strands that flow from the center and each strand is sticky and vibrates when touched;

A spider feels the vibrations when a strand is touched and instantly knows from where on the web the vibrations come;

Once its prey is collected, the spider doesn't have to rush to eat it; it can take its time and come back as often as it needs to eat.

How does the spider analogy compare to inbound marketing?

An effective inbound marketing campaign (Spider Web) is the result of multiple marketing and advertising campaigns that have great Calls-to-Action (Strands). Calls-to-Action are what make your marketing campaigns sticky since your primary goal is to collect contact information. Each time a prospect calls, emails, text messages, fills out a form, attends a conference call, etc., that is a vibration (Notification) that there is an interested prospect.

Your support technology should easily allow you to collect contact information your prospect provides. You can use their contact information to reach out to them multiple times if necessary.

Effective Calls-to-Action combined with good tools and technology allow you to easily identify and collect the contact information of a person that is showing an interest in your product or service.

Inbound Marketing is like a Spider's Web

There are various types of spiders and each type builds a specific type of web – **Marketing Personalities**

A spider usually has bad eyesight and can't chase its prey. Just as you can't always spot which prospect is actually interested in your product/service and which one is wasting your time and effort.

A spider builds its web where it is most likely to catch the type of food it wants to eat – **Triggers/Prospects**

A web has lots of strands – **Multi-Channel Marketing**

Each strand is sticky regardless of which way you go on the web – **Calls-to-Action**

Each strand sends a vibration back to the center of the web to alert a spider that something has disturbed the web – **Data Super Center, Technology, Web Forms, etc.**

A spider's job is to check out whatever made contact with the web – **Prospect Follow-up**

Marketing Personalities

There are 7 Primary Marketing Personalities:

Mailers – Postal mail and email

Writers – Email, letters, articles, blogs, social networking post, books, etc.

Talkers – Telemarketing, face-to-face meetings, vendor booths, conference calls, webinars, door-to-door contact, in-office visits, etc.

Techies – SEO, internet-driven traffic, mobile traffic, YouTube, Facebook, etc.

Networkers – A network of referral partner relationships, networking events, etc.

Traditional Media – television, radio, newspaper, magazines

Non Marketers – They don't perform any types of marketing, they generally rely on customer referrals.

Each person has a dominant marketing personality. That's not to say that you can't or shouldn't be good at multiple types of marketing, but there is always one type that you naturally prefer.

Each business has a dominant marketing personality as well. Often the marketing in a business is influenced by factors and resources (abundant or limited) such as money, technology, and time. This can sometimes force a business to get so focused on one type of marketing that they lose focus of the various types of marketing and advertising campaigns that are available to them.

Another area that limits an individual and a business when it comes to marketing is their M.P.T. The acronym M.P.T. stands for mentality, personality, and technical ability. Mentality is a product of history and is made up of failures, successes, and experiences. Mentality makes you like or dislike certain marketing practices.

Personality is usually based on what is expected to happen in the future and is a product of desires, fears, concerns, insecurities, and strengths. If a person feels that being nice to other people will cause people to be nice to them, they tend to have a good personality. On the other hand, if a person feels like the world is going to screw them over at every turn, they tend to have a crappy personality. Personality plays a key role when selecting the type of marketing campaigns that operate in a business.

If an individual fears that people will be mean and hang up on them if they cold-call a prospect, cold-calling will not happen. If a company fears that they give poor service to their current customers and will get a bunch of bad reviews if they solicit testimonials, a testimonial/review campaign will not happen in the company.

The final letter is T and it stands for technical ability. If the technical ability to operate a marketing campaign doesn't exist in a company, the company usually outsources the marketing campaign or avoids it altogether.

By understanding the M.P.Ts of your company you will better understand why your company chooses to market the way they currently do, instead of deploying all 7 of the primary marketing personalities. By utilizing the marketing campaigns I discuss in this book, a business can better take advantage of the individuals and resources that are available for marketing, and can add a variety of campaigns to its marketing web.

Shopping Triggers

A shopping trigger is a problem, emotion, or situation that makes your product, service, or solution become important to an individual or group. Identifying and utilizing triggers is the primary item that makes a marketing and advertising campaign successful.

Examples of triggers include: insurance policies expiring/renewing, upcoming birthdays, recent relocation, bad weather events, an upcoming special event, upcoming holiday, etc.

You must identify and constantly be on the lookout for the types of triggers that cause people to shop for your product or service.

If a natural trigger doesn't exist for your prospect or customer, you can cause them to become aware of a problem or situation by having a "teachable moment" conversation with them. I teach insurance agents that when they are explaining the various coverage options to a customer or prospect to give them vivid examples of what happens if they get hit by a hit-and-run driver, have a bad weather event come through their town, or get injured on the job, and they don't have the coverage the agent recommends.

Another teachable moment for the prospect or customer I stress to agents is to explain to the prospect/customer how in case of a car accident the medical coverage on an auto policy can be used to fill a gap in their health insurance deductible and co-pay. Their coverage choices can lead to them paying $1000s out of pocket because of the accident, or it can lead to $0.00 out of pocket expenses by choosing the coverage options the agent recommends.

Each profession, and products within that profession, affords a salesperson an opportunity to say "If you don't choose this option, this is something you will have to deal with if this scenario ever happens!" Use this teachable moment to help create an emotional trigger for your prospects/customers.

"Not properly identifying natural shopping triggers or creating an emotional trigger is the #1 reason a marketing campaign is not successful."

Billy R. Williams PhD, 2016 Business.com interview.

Inbound marketing works best when you have consistent marketing and advertising campaigns that key on specific prospect triggers, and each campaign has clear, concise, easy to perform, inbound Calls-to-Action.

Use of non-conventional Calls-to-Action such as: online appointment scheduling tools, text messaging, recorded message marketing, pay-per-quotes, audio/video campaigns, Facebook ads, etc., are great options to add to your currently used Calls-to-Action.

Multi-Channel Marketing

Types of Marketing and Advertising Campaigns you can use:

Live Phone Calls

Emails (manual and drip campaigns)

Mail (postcards & letters)

Door Hangers

On-Line Search Results

Landing Pages

Download Links, Newsletter Sign Up Pop-Up Forms

Social Networking (connections, posts, discussions and responses to questions in online forums or groups)

Blog Posts

Videos - YouTube

Business Referral Partners

Text Message Campaigns (incoming and outgoing)

Recorded Message Marketing

Presentations (live, conference call, webinar)

Car Wraps

Billboards, Bus Benches, Yard Signs

T.V., Radio, Magazines, Press Releases

Books and E-Books

And the list goes on and on!

I could write an entire book just on the various marketing channels that are available to a business today, but instead, I will provide examples of multiple marketing campaigns and channels throughout this book.

Calls-to-Action

A Call-to-Action is the response and/or action that you want the prospect to take after they come in contact with your marketing and advertising campaign. Weak or wrong Calls-to-Action is the #2 reason that marketing and advertising campaigns fail.

Weak Calls-to-Action only give a prospect one primary option to show their interest in your product: "Contact us and let us sell you our product!" While you always want to ask for the sale, you also want to give those folks that are possibly interested in your product, but might not be ready to talk to a sales person, an opportunity to let you know that they have an interest in your product or service. You want them to vibrate a strand on your marketing and advertising web.

A wrong Call-to-Action drives a prospect to a response that either does not show a real interest or does not allow you to collect contact information. The two biggest examples of this that I see are "Like our Facebook page" and "Check out our ad." Facebook has a variety of ad types that will allow you to gather contact information, so look at those campaign options as well, and, unless your ad is a landing page or web form that collects information, that extra step can make a prospect overthink the shopping process and stop dead in their tracks after visiting your ad.

A prospect's shopping psychology is a delicate thing. Give them too much information and they feel empowered because they know a solution to their problem does exist, and now they want to find a cheaper version of that solution. If you don't give them enough information they feel like they are wasting their time on your site or landing page and feel that they need to continue shopping to find the answers or solutions they are searching for.

By providing effective Calls-to-Action, you keep them engaged with you and your solution, and by collecting contact information you can reach out to them and help them determine the best course of action to take to solve their problem. The main intent of your Calls-to-Action should be to collect contact information.

Types of Calls to Action

There are many Call-to-Action types. Here are some examples:

Get a quote by (calling us, emailing us, clicking here, visiting our website, etc.)

Sign up for our newsletter

Click here to download an e-book

Click to call us

Stop by our office

Listen to our short recorded message

Text your email address to receive more information

Watch a video

Email your questions

Complete our online form

Request a quote

Join us on a conference call

Read our latest blog post

Write us a review/testimonial

I will use a variety of Calls-to-Action in the suggested campaigns section of this book.

Inbound Marketing Technology – Data Super Center

Just as each strand sends a vibration back to the center of the web to alert a spider that something has disturbed the web, your marketing technology should make it simple and easy for you to create effective marketing and advertising campaigns that collect contact data and allow you to easily manage that data in one central location.

While there are numerous tools and programs available to you, I want to introduce you to one that I commissioned specifically to fill the void that I was seeing in the inbound marketing space for small businesses. It is called the Data and Marketing Super Center CRM (Automated Marketing Assistant), or Data Super Center for short.

You can locate information on the Data Super Center by visiting www.datasupercenter.org.

If you are an active Inspire a Nation insurance member, Insurance industry-specific Workflows and To-Do Plans (Action Plans) are pre-built for you inside the system, including: entire processes such as the "new customer process," email templates, tasks intervals, landing pages, and auto-responders. (Active Insurance Member Version Only.)

Most small businesses have trouble getting their staff to send the correct email, call back at the right time, or discuss the right web form a customer should complete. Needless to say, this can be a roadblock to your company's success. The Data Super Center allows you to completely automate many of the tasks and conversations that must be in place for your business to grow. You just need to tweak the templates, landing pages, and schedules for your business.

Data Super Center Cost Comparison Chart			
Specific Functionality	Average Monthly Cost	Data Super Center Cost	Data Super Center Function
Low Cost Contact Management Tool	$49.00	Included	Powerful Contact & Data Management
Part Time Receptionist	$500.00	Included	VoiceTouch Automated Receptionist
Dedicated Business Phone Number w/Unlimited Extensions	$40.00	Included	VoiceTouch Automated Receptionist
2 - Way Business Texting	$20.00	Included	Built-In 2-Way Texting Tool
Lead Capturing Landing Pages	$29.00	Included	Unlimited Landing Pages
Drip Email/Autoresponder	$75.00	Included	Max 10K Contacts per Email Blast
Video Email	$49.00	Included	Max 10K Contacts per Email Blast
Recorded Message Marketing Hotline	$10.00	Included	Local or 1-800 Marketing Phone Number
Social Networking Look Up Tool	$15.00	Included	Instantly see your contact's social sites
Professionally Written Newsletter Templates	$49.00	Included	Email, PDF, and Word Templates
Google Calendar Integration	$5.00	Included	One calendar for all your events & Tasks
Total Monthly Cost	$841.00	$74.95	One system that does it all!
	Why Pay This?	Sign Up	

Additional Benefits You Receive When You Sign UP: 10 Minute Business Mentor Video Newsletter, Email and Phone Support

Here are just a few of the features that are part of the Data and Marketing Super Center - Automated Marketing Assistant – www.datasupercenter.org:

The 10 Minute Business Mentor Video Newsletter

We at Inspire a Nation Business Mentoring understand that it is difficult to stay up to date in today's marketing and business environment. That's why we created the 10 Minute Business Mentor Video Series. The training videos will show you step by step how to implement one new marketing process in your business each month! You no longer have to figure out what your next marketing campaign should be. We removed the guess work and give you the detailed, step-by-step, video training you need to get the campaign up and running in your business. Check it out at: http://bit.ly/1OZgKjO.

Lead Capturing Landing Pages

Make your own Landing Pages to capture contact info from your web and mobile visitors. Start with a beautiful template, then customize the wording, decide which data fields to capture, and then publish it on the web. You can do this yourself in a matter of minutes. A contact record with flags and notes is automatically created when a form is completed.

Autoresponders (Drip Emails)

The Data and Marketing Super Center will send your selected email templates on a schedule you choose. You can quickly start and stop autoresponders based on the activity of a contact such as calling into your office, clicking on a link in an email, or sending a text message to your VTAR (VoiceTouch Automated Receptionist).

2-Way Text Messaging

With the Data and Marketing Super Center you will have a text-message-capable phone number. After a contact sends you the initial text message, a contact record is created for them if they don't have an existing record in the system, and you can send 2-way text. The information inside the text messages is captured and retrievable just like an email.

VoiceTouch Automated Receptionist

The Data and Marketing Super Center comes with the VoiceTouch Automated Receptionist. Starting with a local or toll free phone number (you easily select from within the tool), your automated receptionist will create contact records, start or stop tasks and emails, instantly add notes and flags, and allow you to easily link a marketing campaign to one of the unlimited phone extensions we provide. You can also bridge (forward) each extension to the phone number of your choice.

Social Media Integration

The Data and Marketing Super Center will automatically search the web for your contact's social media profiles based on the email address inside the system and then display the results right there next to your contact's photo. Just add their email address, and Social Connector will do the rest.

Easy Contact Filtering

OK, so you have 5000 contacts in your database...now what? Imagine if you could filter that list by "Hot Prospect", or "Former Customer" or "Likes heavy starch" or "Loves Dogs," etc... You get the idea. In the Data and Marketing Super Center you can categorize and flag your clients anyway you want to, create your own custom fields, and then easily sort and segment your list in seconds.

A Monthly Newsletter that is ready to send to your contacts

Each month a new newsletter is added to your system that is professionally designed and ready to send to your contacts. The newsletters have topics such as "Recipe of the Month," "Brain Teasers," and other interesting topics.

Google Calendar Integration

Keep track of your appointments in our easy-to-use Google integrated calendar. See daily, weekly and monthly views, drag and drop appointments, and even see and view your contacts from within the calendar.

Easy Mail and Email Merge

Ever try to mail-merge your contact info into a letter in Excel or Word? The Data and Marketing Super Center makes this process super simple. Your letters and emails look professional, custom, and you can do it yourself in seconds.

Video Email

Stand out from the crowd by sending Video Emails. Video Emails are considerably more effective than traditional emails. The Data and Marketing Super Center makes creating and sending Video Emails Super Simple.

Agenda Assistant

With the Agenda Assistant, the Data and Marketing Super Center will send you an email each morning to tell you when you have appointments, tasks to complete, client birthdays, and more.

Birthday Assistant

Remembering your clients' birthdays is a great way to show you really care about them on a personal level. The Birthday Assistant will automatically send your client a birthday email or set up a task to remind you of this important event.

As we said, this is only a few of the features that are part of the Data and Marketing Super Center!

We will use the functionality of the Data Super Center for our marketing examples throughout this book. If you already have a system or tool(s) that allows you to perform and track the campaigns we will discuss in a few minutes, use that system or tool(s) to implement the campaigns.

Designing an Inbound Marketing and Advertising Campaign

Designing an inbound marketing campaign is a very simple process. It has 7 main components:

The Problem - Emotional Trigger

Target Prospects – The type, demographic, or niche prospect

Marketing Campaign – The type of marketing or advertising campaign you will use

Inbound Call to Action - Desired response

Marketing Tools Needed – Data Super Center or other marketing tools

Implementation Day/Time – Self-explanatory

Schedule – How often will you perform this marketing campaign? Usually this is determined by the success of previous marketing campaigns of this type.

Another way of putting it is:

What problem does my product or service solve?

Who is experiencing the problem that emotionally triggers the desire for my product or solution?

What marketing campaigns can I use to reach them?

What do I want them to do after they get my marketing campaign?

What tools do I need to get this campaign up and running?

What day and time will I implement the marketing campaign?

How often will I run this marketing campaign?

We find that by starting with a visual or written outline of the campaign it is easier to: design the marketing campaign, easier to choose the marketing materials and resources you will need, and easier to explain the marketing campaign to other people.

Example Marketing Campaigns - Written Outline

Problem – Emotional Trigger: upcoming birthday

Target Prospect(s): current customer

Marketing Campaign(s): life insurance email blast, life insurance postal mailing

Inbound Call to Action: call us, email us, complete out a short life insurance quote form

Marketing Tools and Resources Needed: Data Super Center email and letter templates, Data Super Center Pre-built landing page

Implementation Day/Time: Monday/11:00 a.m.

Schedule: 10 days before customer birthday.

Below is a visual display of a New Customer To-Do Plan in the Data and Marketing Super Center.

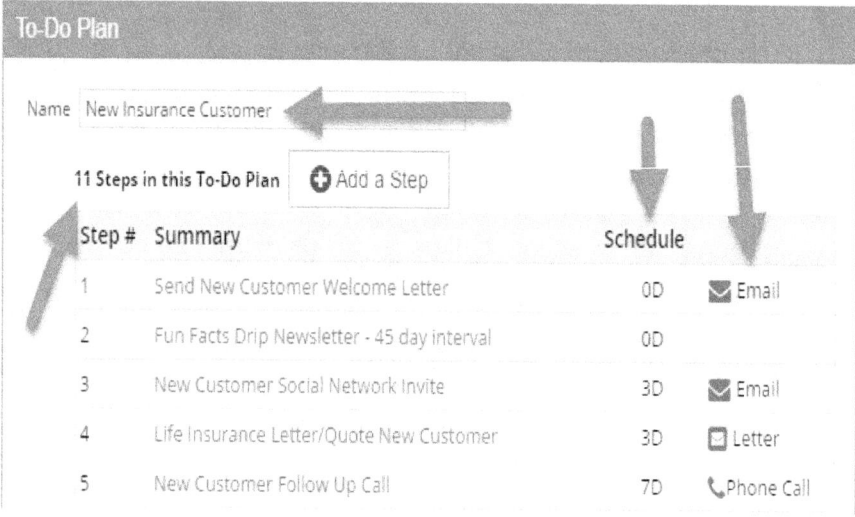

Steps to Create a Marketing Campaign

Step 1: Identify a problem, situation, or event that emotionally triggers a need for your product or service. Note: If your product does not have strong emotional triggers associated with it, you must use teachable moments within your marketing to create an emotional trigger. We will give you some examples in the suggested campaign section of this book.

Step 2: Identify various target prospects. This can be a list of current customers, a purchased list of prospects, a specific target demographic (age, income, gender, etc.), a geographic area, or any other way you choose to segment your target prospect. The 5 Best Prospects examples provided below is a good place to start.

Step 3: Identify the different marketing campaigns available to your business. The main campaigns that businesses use are: referrals, email, mail, telemarketing, social networking, and advertising; however, there are many other options available to your business.

Step 4: Identify your desired Call-to-Action: Have a clear vision of what you want the prospect to do after they receive your marketing campaign. This step is generally the area where most businesses drop the ball. Give your prospects choices other than "Call, email me, or stop by my business during our normal business hours." Make sure that you use Calls-to-Action that collect contact information.

Step 5: Setup all tools and resources that will allow your prospect to complete your desired call to action. This could include: placing a quote box on your website, setting up a recorded message, signing up for a conference call number, signing up for a testimonial review site, or attaching a document to a download form on your social networking sites. If you are using the Data Super Center, the majority of the Call-to-Action functions are built into the system.

Step 6: Choose a specific day and time to start the marketing campaign. Your marketing campaigns have a much greater chance of happening if there is a designated implementation day and time on your calendar!

Step 7: Select the schedule of the campaign: Some campaigns will happen as a part of technology such as drip email and will occur on a regular basis, while other campaigns might only happen once a year. It is important that you understand the desired schedule of your marketing campaigns.

There are other items you have to take into consideration such as who will perform the marketing or Prospecting? What tools or technology is needed? And, what tracking tools will be used? Generally those questions are answered as you set up the marketing campaigns. Just by getting through the 7 core steps you will understand what campaigns will work for your business and which ones will not work.

The 5 Best Prospects and examples of campaigns you can use

Prospect 1: Prospects that have shown an interest in acquiring your product: Contacts that called, emailed, stopped by the office, filled out a web form or landing page, attended a workshop, webinar, or conference call, requested information on a forum or blog, started a chat or text message conversation with the business, responded to a marketing email/mailing/phone call, etc.

Prospect 2: Customers or Prospects from another professional or business that recommends and endorses you: Existing referral relationships, former referral relationships that fell off the map, LinkedIn connections, someone that featured your company, product, or service in an online write-up, resource partners, joint presenters at a live meeting, workshop, conference call, or webinar sponsored or endorsed by the professional or business; etc.

Prospect 3: Prospects that have a possible upcoming need for your product: Upcoming expiration or renewal date, prior conversation about your product, prospect matches criteria such as credit score, age, 20-mile radius, business owner, recent or upcoming event such as birthday, new baby, newly married, newly divorced, new movers, etc.

Prospect 4: Your Current Customers: Upcoming birthday contact process, upcoming customer renewals, testimonial request, referral request, new customer onboarding process, emergency contact process, product weakness conversations, "we haven't talked in a while" outreach, etc.

Prospect 5: Prospects or customers that bought your product in the past: Former customer win-back campaigns, a purchased list of customers that bought your product from you or a competitor, someone that left a comment on a review site or social networking post.

I don't have the money to market and advertise my business!

I hear this statement all the time and this is always my response: "There are too many free and low-cost ways for you to market and advertise your business to continue to use that excuse."

Between the internet, social networking, and an onslaught of low-cost technology tools available to a business owner today, there really is no viable excuse to sit on the marketing sidelines.

The main 3 factors I see that cause businesses to not take advantage of all of the options available to them today are:

1. Ignorance – Often they don't try to find out what low-cost options are available to their businesses;

2. Fear – Fear of learning a new technology, or just the plain fear of doing something different can cause paralysis by analysis; and,

3. Lack of discipline – Mental, physical, and emotional

Let's look at discipline - 3 types of discipline are necessary to grow a business:

Self-Discipline – Doing what you need to do, when you need to do it, in the way it needs to be done.

Accountability – The use of accountability meetings, tools, and technology to hold the employees of the business accountable for their actions and conversations.

Outsourcing – If you won't do, and you won't make your employees do it, but it needs to be done for your business to grow, then outsource it to someone or something else. Often the increased income will more than justify the expense of outsourcing it. This is especially true for low-cost technology.

Discipline and Money

Self-Discipline and Money – The more disciplined you are about your business, the more attention you pay to information that impacts your business and the more buttons and tabs you are willing to push in the technology that is used in your business. Self-disciplined business owners tend to spend less money overall than their peers.

Accountability and Money – The more you hold yourself and your employees accountable for tasks, the more total tasks you can implement in the business, and the more efficient the business becomes overall. The less accountability there is, the more dependent the business becomes on the self-discipline of the employees. This generally forces the business owner to have to pay a higher base salary than their peers. Less accountability = higher employee pay and less continuity in the business.

Outsourcing and Money – The less disciplined the leader is the more money the business has to spend on outsourcing to stay average with its peers. Disciplined leaders use outsourcing to stay ahead of their peers.

Why did I take the rabbit trail on discipline in a business? Because in my opinion it is the business leader's lack of business discipline and staff accountability that dooms most small businesses.

I can fill this book with great marketing and Call-to-Action ideas and plans, but if they are never implemented then my words and wisdom can't have a real impact in your business.

Low-Cost Options to Traditional (Expensive) Marketing and Advertising Platforms

Television Commercials - YouTube, Facebook Video, and Google

Radio Advertising - iTunes, Internet Radio, MP3 Audio Files

Book Publishing - Amazon, LULU.com, Google Books

Live Meetings/Conference - Webinars and Conference Calls

Postal Mail - Facebook Ads, Business Referral Partners, Google Ads

Billboards - Yard Signs, Flyers, Banners, Car Wraps

Newspapers Advertising - Social Networks, Mobile Apps, Blogs

Paid Referrals - Online Reviews and Testimonials

Outbound Sales Team - Email, Recorded Message Marketing, Text Message Marketing

Suggested Marketing and Advertising Campaigns

Modify these suggested marketing campaigns to match the marketing personality, resources, and technology in your business. I am going to give you a specific marketing campaign but you can modify most of the campaigns to fit any marketing channel. Examples of this include: sending postal mail instead of writing a blog post, or sending an email along with an auto-dialer call to a business phone number instead of a Facebook ad. The more multi-channel you make your marketing campaigns, the more inbound traffic you will generate.

Never lose focus of the fact that it is the Call-to-Action that makes an inbound marketing campaign successful. With the right inbound Calls-to-Action any marketing and advertising campaign can drive inbound prospects.

Let's start off with a fairly simple campaign.

Campaign – Upcoming Insurance Renewal

Trigger: upcoming insurance renewal

Target Prospects: former customers, purchased expiration date list

Marketing Campaign: postal mail and an email blast

Inbound Call-to-Action: call the agency, come by our office, or schedule an appointment

Inbound Call-to-Action Wording: "Our records show your home insurance is about to expire. Call or come by our office and allow us to quote your auto and home and have a short conversation with you about the quote, and we will give you a $25.00 restaurant.com gift certificate for your time. You can use our online calendar to schedule an appointment."

Marketing Tools: Data Super Center email templates, postal letter templates, appointment landing page functionality, and built-in call tracking phone number. You can also use an online scheduling tool we use on a regular basis called simplybook.me instead of the Data Super Center appointment landing page.

Summary: This type of campaign should be easy to implement. Mailers and writers usually do well with this campaign type. Modify this campaign for your product and/or service. If you need to purchase a marketing list please look at the Inspire a Nation Recommended Vendors Page - http://www.inspireanation.org/recommended-vendors.

On the campaign above I showed the trigger and target prospects; however, each business and product will have a unique trigger, a unique target prospect, and a best time/day to reach them. So for the remaining suggested campaigns I will leave off the trigger and target prospect fields. I will leave the implementation day/time and schedule up to you.

Let's look at campaigns you can modify for your business

Campaign 1 – Testimonial/Review Request

Marketing Campaign: Email blast and/or a conversation with current customers

Inbound Call-to-Action: Write a nice review or testimonial for our business

Inbound Call-to-Action Wording: Please help us by letting others who are searching for (the primary product(s) you offer) know that we provide exceptional service. You can do this by writing a positive review/testimonial on our Google Search Result Listing. To do this for me, simply:

1. Search on Google for us by name (your business name),

2. On the right side of the Google page you will see a map to our location and possibly a picture. You should also see a "Write a Review Button," and

3. Please write us a positive review and email a copy to us

<u>Marketing Tools:</u> Data Super Center for customer contact information storage and the email blast, or you can use a tool like Mail Chimp, IContact, or Constant Contact.

You must have registered your business on Google https://www.google.com/business/. Make sure you respond to any negative comments with an apology and a solution addressing the problem.

Yelp is an alternative to Google Reviews, but, in my opinion, because of Google's place in the search engine world, and because of the SEO benefits you get, Google Reviews should be your number one choice, followed by sites such as Yelp, Amazon, YP.com, and others.

The overall best option is to give your customers multiple review site choices. Here is wording you can use:

Please take a moment to write a short positive review or comment about our company that we can post on our website and share with others who are trying to find out more information about our products and services.

Long or short, your comments are very valuable to us.

Thank you in advance for your time and your kind words.

There are several ways to post your comments to us:

1. Post them on Google + by locating us by name on a Google Search (i.e., ABC Company). On the right side of the search results you will see a map to our location. In the box with the map is a "write a review" link. Log in, and post your review;

2. Post them on your personal Facebook page and please email us a copy;

3. Email them to us at (email@myemailaddress.com); or

4. Call us and share your kind words with one of our team members at (your phone number).

Another form of a testimonial is getting your customer to put a yard sign in their front yard for a week or two promoting your business. A yard sign will work for most businesses, but for some reason it is generally used by roofing contractors, pool installation companies, and real estate agents.

Campaign 2 – Pay per Quote (Non-Profits)

Marketing Campaign: A letter to non-profit representatives and/or live office visit

Inbound Call to Action: My company will donate $?? For every household from your organization that allows us to quote their home and auto insurance

Inbound Call-to-Action Wording: Hi this is (your name) with (your company). My company will donate $?? For every household from your organization that allows us to quote their home and auto insurance. No purchase is necessary to receive our donation. I know that fundraising is a major concern for most non-profit groups, just as getting new customers is a concern for my company. This program is a win-win for both of us. To discuss this program with me, simply call me at (your phone number), email me at (your email) or stop by my office at (your address). I look forward to speaking with a rep from your non-profit group.

Marketing Tools: Data Super Center – Letter Templates and Call Tracking Number. You can also send a postcard from a company like Post Card Mania and use your regular phone number.

If you are an insurance agent you should check out the Inspire a Nation Business Mentoring Insurance Agent Mentoring Program (http://www.inspireanation.org/membershipinformation). We provide insurance-specific templates, role play examples and mentoring guidance.

A pay-per-quote campaign is a great way to pick up high-quality leads from within a specific group or niche. As with all marketing, your donations to non-profit organizations is tax deductible. This is also a great way to get name recognition with the community and local corporate "movers and shakers" as this is usually who sits on non-profit boards.

Campaign 3 – Conference Call Presentation

Marketing Campaign: You can use mail, email, postal letters, flyers, social networking posts, inbound text messaging, etc., to promote your conference call

Inbound Call-to-Action: Sign up and attend our conference call

Inbound Call-to-Action Wording: Attend our short conference call and learn what is available to solve the top two issues (triggers) that are on the minds of (target prospect). To accommodate your schedule the call will be held at 12 noon and 6:30 p.m. on (date). Here is the call-in information.

Marketing Tools: Data Super Center – Contact info storage, email blast, postal letter template, landing page (if you want contacts to register using a landing page. It reduces the total number of sign-ups, but the lead quality is greatly increased), inbound text messaging (you can ask the contact to text their email address to your Data Super Center text message number and they will receive an auto-response email with the conference call information).

Use www.freeconferencecall.com to conduct and record the actual conference call. www.freeconferencecall.com will also give you a saved recording call-in number that makes the recording available

24x7. You can also promote the recorded session by putting the recorded message call-in number on your website and on your marketing materials.

Campaign 4 – Car Wrap Signage

Marketing Campaign: People will see your car wrap as you drive around

Inbound Call-to-Action: Text message your email address to receive instant information

Inbound Call-to-Action Wording: Are you interested in finding out more info about (product or service)? Call me at (phone number) or text message your email address to (Data Super Center inbound text message number) and receive instant information.

Marketing Tools: Data Super Center inbound text message number.

You can also use a text messaging tool like betwext, biztexter, or EZTexting. Use a local shop to produce your car wrap. Use can also use a magnetic sign, but only if you will not travel at high speeds in your vehicle.

Campaign 5 – Promotional Items

Marketing Campaign: Giveaways such as pens, key chains, water bottles, etc.

Inbound Call-to-Action: Use a QR Code to increase inbound traffic

Inbound Call-to-Action Wording: Call (phone number) or scan to schedule an appointment

Marketing Tools: Data Super Center – Call tracking phone number and appointment request landing page.

You can use a national company like Vistaprint, or, a local vendor to purchase promotional items.

A recorded message phone number, text message option, QR Codes, and a video link are creative options you can use.

Campaign 6 – Downloadable Report

Enter your name:

Enter your email:

Get Access Today!

Marketing Campaign: Social Networking and Blog Post

Inbound Call-to-Action: Download our special report

Inbound Call-to-Action Wording: There is a lot of misinformation floating around about (trigger topic). If you want real answers to real questions download our special report.

Marketing Tools: Data Super Center – landing page with autoresponder functionality. You can also use a squeeze page on your existing website, or a landing page creation tool like Leadpages.

Make sure that your special report is not just a glorified sales catalog and that it really does contain useful information. That is not to say that it needs to be a Harvard Business School research paper, just a well written, quality content filled report, white paper, or brochure.

Of course you must be set up on social networking sites such as Facebook for business, LinkedIn, and/or a company blog. You can also post to groups and communities on Facebook, LinkedIn, and Google Communities.

You generally get a much greater response when you post to sites or groups where the users are engaged and active.

Instagram and Pinterest are options as well.

If you have Business Referral Partners make sure they have links and download tabs for your downloadable reports as well.

Campaign 7 – Text Message Campaign

Marketing Campaign: Inbound Calls-to-Action wording on your website and social networking sites, as well as an email blast to all of your contacts

Inbound Call-to-Action: Text message your email address

Inbound Call-to-Action Wording: "If you would like to receive a free copy of my latest E-Book "How 2 Make Your Business a Magnet for Inbound Prospects" simply text message your email address to 682-200-1808."

Marketing Tools: Data Super Center inbound text message number. You can also use a text messaging tool like betwext, biztexter, or EZTexting.

This is by far my number one marketing campaign for promoting new books I write. It is clean, quick, and easy. To send out the free copy of the E-Book all I have to do is send out an email blast using the Data Super Center with a direct link to Amazon. This is how I drive my books to #1 on Amazon before I actually start charging for the book.

To add yourself to receive a free copy of any books I will release in the future, text your email address to 682-200-1808 or download our mobile app: https://inspireanationmentoring.appsme.com.

You can use text message campaigns in a variety of ways. Use it for newsletter signups, to send promotional coupons, and to remind customers and prospects of upcoming appointments.

Just remember the contact has to text in first, and you should ask them to text in their email address.

Campaign 8 – Mobile App Download Campaign

Marketing Campaign: Promote a mobile app for your business by using a variety of marketing channels

Inbound Call-to-Action: Download our mobile app

Inbound Call-to-Action Wording: Download our mobile app and receive discount coupons, schedule appointments through the app, and be the first to know about new products and services. Download our app by using this link: (Example: https://inspireanationmentoring.appsme.com).

Marketing Tools: Data Super Center – Email blast, text message auto response, landing pages, and special call-in tracking number.

At one time a mobile app was the unicorn of marketing for small businesses. Now companies like appsme.com make it easy and affordable for any small business to have an app. Features like click-through email and phone number links make it simple and easy for people to contact you using the app. Other features like "push notifications" allow you to send notices and messages directly to a person's mobile device. Small businesses tend to see a low volume of app downloads compared to the fun and game apps available, but the engagement factor outweighs the low volume.

Campaign 9 – Birthday Club Registration

Marketing Campaign: Birthday Club website page or landing page

Inbound Call-to-Action: Sign-up for our Birthday Club

Inbound Call-to-Action Wording: We know your birthday is a special day and we want to help make it even more special. Register for birthday rewards by completing our short form.

Marketing Tools: Data Super Center – Birthday Assistant function, birthday letter template, autoresponder (drip email), email blast, and landing page.

A birthday is an awesome time to communicate with your customers, prospects, and general contacts. A process that we teach at Inspire a Nation Business Mentoring is to write a contact's birth day and month (don't ask for the year) on the back of their business card when the contact gives you a business card, and then, load the contact info and birthday into an automated tool that sends a drip email or prewritten text message on their birthday. For retail businesses this is a great time to offer discounts or special gifts.

The Birthday Club Sign-up landing page should be festive and inviting. When a person sees the form on the landing page it should look and feel special enough to make them want to provide their contact information. Always ask for the mobile number and permission to text message on the form.

The Data Super Center's Birthday Assistant function automatically sends out a birthday email to a contact on or before their birthday if their contact record has a valid email address and their birthdate is on their contact record. The contact completing the Data Super Center Birthday Club landing page automatically triggers the Birthday Assistant Function.

In addition to the Data Super Center you can create a Birthday Club landing page on your website or blog, or you can provide a signup link in your emails and postal mailings.

Bdayfreeday.com is a great site to check out the birthday clubs of major corporations.

Campaign 10 – Information Webinar

Marketing Campaign: Multi-channel promotion. Use as many marketing channels as possible

Inbound Call-to-Action: Sign-up and attend our upcoming webinar

Inbound Call-to-Action Wording: Sign-up and attend our short webinar to learn how we solve the ??? (problem) for our customers.

Marketing Tools: Data Super Center – Landing Page and autoresponder email campaign to send initial confirmation emails and reminder emails.

There are a ton of web meeting tools available to you. The 3 that we recommend are: AnyMeeting, Freescreensharing, and GotoMeeting. Use this comparison site to compare multiple web meeting vendors side-by-side: http://www.capterra.com/web-conferencing-software/.

Webinars are the marketing campaign of choice today for many midsize and large companies. Webinars allow the presenters to have a semi-captive and semi-engaged audience. Most importantly it allows the companies that host the webinars to collect an accurate email address, and about 40% of the time, an accurate phone number. Always use multi-channel promotions with your webinars. An email blast seems to always provide the best sign-up returns, but the webinar sign-up link should be on your website, social networking sites, and blog posts. If you conduct a regularly scheduled webinar be sure to have a poster or flyer in your office with a QR Code or text message with autoresponder capabilities.

One-on-One and small group webinars are great for sales conversations, service conversations, and hiring interviews. I am a huge fan of webinars (live and recorded) and I conduct a free training/mentoring webinar every two weeks for small businesses: http://www.inspireanation.org/bi-weekly-training-sign-up, and I record and post a monthly web newsletter called the "10 Minute Business Mentor: http://www.inspireanation.org/10-Minute-Business-Mentor-Videos.

Campaign 11 – SEO/Keyword/Key Phrase/Metadata

<u>Marketing Campaign:</u> SEO/Keyword/Key Phrase/Metadata

I am going to cut straight to the bone on this topic. When it comes to SEO I have read tons of books and worked with some of the top SEO companies in the field. My suggestion is to work with a company that specializes in local SEO. Two companies I recommend are: www.web.com and https://www.aabacosmallbusiness.com/ for local SEO, and a book called SEO 2016 https://amzn.com/B00NH0XZR0 if you want a great book on SEO.

I don't want to leave you totally high and dry on this topic, so check out Campaign 25 (Search Result Marketing) for more specific information and instruction.

Campaign 12 – Video Email Campaign

Marketing Campaign: Video email blast to your contacts

Inbound Call-to-Action: Click here to see our short video

Inbound Call-to-Action Wording: We took the time to create a short video that will answer many of the questions you might have about ?? (a problem the contact has, or, a solution you provide).

Marketing Tools: Data Super Center – Video email templates and call-in tracking phone number. YouTube is always the recommended place to host your video because of the SEO impact.

If you use a 3rd party video email solution, make sure the video actually plays inside of the email. Many 3rd party video email providers simply hide a YouTube link behind a JPEG picture and your contact will end up on YouTube to watch the video, and you know how easy it is to get distracted with all the video thumbnails showing beside your video.

Your video doesn't have to be professionally shot to be effective. It can be as simple as you using the webcam on your tablet, or the camera on your phone to discuss the problems you solve for your customers and the tools and solutions you use to solve those problems. If you don't want live video footage, a slide show with voice over will do just fine.

Campaign 13 – Recorded Message Campaign

Marketing Campaign: Multi-channel promotion. Use as many marketing channels as possible.

Inbound Call-to-Action: Call our job hotline and listen to the job description for the available sales position

Inbound Call-to-Action Wording: Call our job hotline 123-456-7890 and listen to a job description of our open sales position.

Marketing Tools: Data Super Center – Use one of the unlimited extensions available with the Data Super Center call-in tracking number to record job descriptions, sales messages, promotional audio, and other audio recordings. In addition, you can upload a prerecorded MP3 file. The Data Super Center can automatically start or stop drip email campaigns, to-do campaigns, and workflow task for contacts already in the database, as well as automatically create a contact record using the phone number of the contact.

Like video marketing, audio marketing is a nice change to written content. When a link to audio is received in an email or clicked when on a website or landing page, it automatically plays using the speakers on a mobile device or computer. Listening to audio is similar to listening to a radio and doesn't require that a person completely stop tasks they were trying to complete.

You can also use tools like free conference call, Facebook (load your MP3 files), and your website to store audio files and give hyperlink access to your contacts.

You can use the audio recorder on your mobile device or a tool like Audacity from SourceForge.net to record MP3 audio.

https://sourceforge.net/projects/audacity/

Campaign 14 – Business Referral Partner Recruiting Campaign

Marketing Campaign: Send a Business Referral Partner prospecting letter to selected professionals

Inbound Call-to-Action: Call or email me to discuss referrals

Inbound Call-to-Action Wording: I am looking to start a referral partnership with local (select a profession). I would like to schedule a time with you to see if we would be a good fit. Here is a link to my online calendar. Please select a time and day that best fits your schedule and I will contact you. Prior to our conversation, please take a moment and review testimonials and reviews that our customers have provided about our service. Here is the link: testimonials@yourwebsite.com.

Marketing Tools: Data Super Center – Letter templates, appointment landing page, call tracking number. You can also use an online appointment tool like simplybook.me to allow your referral partner prospect to schedule an appointment. Use sites like whitepages.com, yellowpages.com, Google, and LinkedIn to locate the mailing addresses (and sometimes the email addresses) of your prospects.

Professional referral partnerships should be a foundational way of driving prospects to your small business. The process is very simple: 1. Identify the type of professionals that support the type of prospects you need for your business, 2. Locate contact information for your referral partner prospect on one of the sites mentioned above, 3. Mail them a Business Referral Partner prospect letter with a hyperlink to an online appointment tool and a hyperlink to testimonials and reviews about your business. This can be a link to your Google reviews, your website, or a site like Yelp.

We recommend you send a letter to 5 or more people of the same profession that don't house in the same office. While some people would consider it cold calling, we recommend that if you have not heard from the referral prospects that you sent a letter after 10 business days, that you call them to make sure they are still in business. If you happen to get them on the phone, let them know that you mailed a referral partner letter to them, and let them know the type of relationship you are trying to establish.

Social Networking Section

Yes, social networking is so important and has so many options available to you that it needs its own section in this book.

I will look at four specific ways to use social networking to help drive inbound prospects: personal connections, joining an existing social networking group, writing updates and posts, and finally starting a social networking group that you own.

You should treat your social network community the same way you would treat individuals and professional connections within your local community. You have to identify:

1. Current Customers that have an active social network profile,

2. Professionals that you think can benefit your business,

3. Professionals and groups that can send you referrals,

4. Professional groups and niches that you want to target as prospects, and

5. Professionals and groups that can help keep you up to date on your professional education.

Another great benefit of social networking that you should take advantage of is called "Social Listening."

Social Listening is where you look for triggers in the conversations, updates, and posts of your contacts and groups. There are businesses that thrive on social listening. It is a great low-cost way of getting leads. If you are a small business on a tight budget, the social networking campaigns I am about to explain along with Social Triggers should be a part of your marketing tool kit.

Campaign 15 – Social Networking – Personal Connections

Marketing Campaign: Send a connection request to all of your current contacts and any new contacts you meet

Inbound Call-to-Action: Connect with me on (social networking site)

Inbound Call-to-Action Wording: Your business profile is impressive to me and I would like to add you to my professional network.

Marketing Tools: Data Super Center – Social Connector feature, data management function, email function, and inbound call tracking. Other tools available to you include social networking management tools like Hootsuite, Hearsay Social, and Buffer.

Growing your personal and professional networks should be a major part of growing your brand, reputation, and business. Today's social networking environment and tools make it easy to connect with your contacts via social networking platforms. Every time you meet someone and you get their business card or contact information presents an opportunity for you to reach out to connect with them via social networking. The Data Super Center has a feature called Social Connector that instantly searches the internet to match the email address loaded into the data supercenter with social networking profiles that use the same email address. Once located, with one click of a button you can ask to connect with the contact.

Where most small businesses struggle is in figuring out how to maximize connections without abusing the relationship by sending them spam messages or information that is unimportant to the connection. You can never completely predict what is important to your connection, however, you can control spamming your connection.

Once connected, send an introduction message that explains your expertise, identifies one major problem that you solve for your customers, and provides your contact information. This will let the contact understand what you do professionally, and it will give you a chance to showcase your product in a way that is professional but not spammy.

Here is wording that we recommend you modify and use: *Thank you for connecting with me. My expertise is helping folks to (insert your business focus here, i.e., understand their Medicare Advantage options, choose the best retirement options, select coverage that will best protect their quality of life should they have an at-fault auto accident, etc.), and from time to time I plan to post some interesting articles and information on my updates.*

If you have questions that you feel my expertise can answer for you, a customer of yours, or a group or organization that you are a part of, here is my direct contact information:

Name:

Email:

Testimonials page of my website

Work phone

I am usually available Monday – Friday 8:30 AM – 5:30 PM and Saturday 9:00 a.m. – 1:00 p.m.

Every week or two post something that you write, or a link to an interesting article/blog post that you discovered, in your profile update. If you have information that you feel would be useful for a specific contact, or a specific group of contacts, send the information as a private email instead of a public post.

Use the birthday notices provided by most social networking sites to send a private birthday message to your contacts. I strongly recommend that you DO NOT send the canned quick responses provided by LinkedIn and other social networking platforms on birthdays, job anniversaries, etc. Your contact will receive dozens of these canned responses and will start to ignore them after the first 5 or 6 they receive.

Every 30 days you need to download all of your contact's information from the various social networking platforms and add it to your business database system (Data Super Center). Not all sites will allow you to download contact info, and I can easily predict that some sites that currently allow it will change their policy in the near future as the pressure to produce more advertising revenues increase. I personally download my LinkedIn contacts every 30 days and I add them to any newsletter or email blast I have set up.

Campaign 16 – Join an Existing Social Networking Group

Marketing Campaign: Join an existing social networking group

Inbound Call-to-Action: Introduction wording below, responses to existing discussions, questions you submit to the group

Inbound Call-to-Action Wording: Based on the conversation and responses.

Marketing Tools: What? Billy, you are not going to lead with the Data Super Center? You will use the Data Super Center when you download and store your social network contact's information, but you will use the actual social network platform to join groups and engage with the groups.

Joining groups allows you to meet:

Professionals that you think can benefit your business,

Professionals and groups that can send you referrals,

Professional groups and niches that you want to target as prospects,

Professionals and groups that can help keep you up to date on your professional education.

In addition, on LinkedIn, when you and a contact share a group, you can connect to them without providing an email address or having to be introduced to them by one of your other connections.

The key to being a rock star in a social networking group is not by posting the most, but by adding value to existing discussions through your comments, answers to questions, and providing links to resources such as other sites that provide answers. If your answers lead them to your products and services not because you are just trying to push your products, but because you truly are the expert and your products and services are the best solution, you will be not only accepted but lauded by other group members.

Once you have added value at least 5 times to group discussions, go ahead and write an update that shows how a customer's life was improved when they had your product at a critical moment, and how another person or customer's life was much more complicated when they didn't have your product or service at a critical time. The 5 value to 1 promotion ratio works well most of the time.

Campaign 17 – Social Network Updates and Posts

Marketing Campaign: Social Network Updates and Posts

Inbound Call-to-Action: Based on the update and/or post

Inbound Call-to-Action Wording: Based on the update and/or post

Marketing Tools: Data Super Center – Inbound call tracking, inbound text messaging, landing pages and web forms, and autoresponder features. Every 5th update or post should drive inbound prospects.

You can use your social network sites as an additional blog. In addition, by linking all of your social sites, you can easily update multiple sites at the same time.

LinkedIn Pulse is a great option for writing articles, but there are some specialty and niche social networking sites that give you a lot of bang for the buck. The ones that jump out at me most are: Quora, Reddit, and Digg. Of course every profession has its own blog site or journal that is the go to source for that profession. Try your best to get published by your industry's best online resources.

While at it, don't forget your Facebook Groups and Google Communities. These are additional free resources that you can use to post your articles, updates, and blog posts.

To spice up your updates and posts, add hyperlinks, video, audio, graphics, and contact information.

Campaign 18 – Start Your Own Social Networking Group

Marketing Campaign: Start your own social networking group

Inbound Call-to-Action: Join our??? group

Inbound Call-to-Action Wording: Join our ??? group and interact with other like-minded individuals that are excited about ??? (the main focus of the group).

Marketing Tools: Various social networking sites and platforms

This campaign works especially well for writers and techies. Starting and owning a group not only gives you control of the content that is posted, but it allows you access to the contact information of group members. You can blast notices to the group, and you can control others who are trying to take over the group with spammy post and links.

A group is a great way to start and moderate a Q and A forum for a specific niche. A Q and A forum allows you to really keep your "ear to the ground" when it comes to your industry, product, or service.

Some group owners start a group and then allow the group to grow on its own with no real controls or moderation of the group. Generally the less control you exert over a group the larger it will grow since nothing is in place to stop anyone from posting anything.

For a higher quality group, I suggest you have some sort of moderation in place. The easiest way is to have sub categories within your group such as: marketing, discussions, promotions, events, etc. This gives your group members a place to promote their products or events, and makes it easy for the people that are interested in the content to find it, without everyone in the group being exposed to it.

In addition, if you have a sales team that monitors the group, you can pick up some pretty good leads.

Additional Marketing and Advertising Campaigns

Campaign 19 – Local Media Coverage

Marketing Campaign: Submit an article or news story to local media

Inbound Call-to-Action: Possible story for your newsfeed

Inbound Call-to-Action Wording: "I've noticed there has been a lot of buzz around the topic of ????. I've dealt with this issue many times within my professional career and I have some insight that I believe can add a layer of detail and value that your audience would greatly appreciate."

Marketing Tools: Google search, Data Super Center – Letter template, email template, contact management, social networking, and postal mail.

We all know the power and influence media can have on our business. One good profile story on a local television broadcast or in a local or national newspaper can drive your business to new heights. They key is how to get your name and expertise in front of local media. Here are steps I recommend:

1. Use the following search key to locate local media – News+reporter+City, State. If you want to really refine your search

of reporters and journalists, use a specific keyword in your search such as: news+business reporter+City, State. Usually this will lead you to the website of all local stations. These websites generally have profiles with email addresses of all their reporters. Use the email addresses and other provided contact information to send your idea for a story.

2. Reach out to your media contacts and ask them to profile a specific topic or situation that is currently in the news cycle and use your insight and experience in their story.

3. You MUST offer a viewpoint, perspective, or action plan that adds value to the viewer, listener, or reader. Simply stating that you sell a solution is not the type of value reporters are looking for. Use specific experience and testimonials from customers to offer credibility and support for your knowledge and wisdom.

4. Use the birthday campaign explained above to keep in touch with your contacts.

5. Connect with the reporters on social networking.

6. Regularly submit an idea to the reporter/journalist. As they get to know you better, they are more likely to use you as a source when a source is needed for a story or topic.

While this process requires more outbound outreach that many of the other campaigns, the return can often trump all of the other campaigns combined!

Campaign 20 – Live Events with Free Display Booths

<u>Marketing Campaign:</u> Live Events with Free Display Booths

<u>Inbound Call-to-Action:</u> Display your business at no cost at our upcoming live event

<u>Inbound Call-to-Action Wording:</u> On Saturday ??/??/???? come out and display your business, (For Free!) at our local small business expo. Each business will receive a 6 x 6 space (as an example) to show off their products and services. Call ???-???-???? or, email info@yourdomain.com for more information.

Marketing Tools: Data Super Center – Contact management, email template, letter template, landing page (space registration), email autoresponder reminders and event registration confirmation, inbound call tracking. You can also use a registration site and tool such as Eventbrite, Eventzilla, Evite, and Picatic. Of the ones I just named that are not named Data Super Center, I like Eventbrite and Picatic the best.

This type of marketing campaign works well if you have a dedicated space that you will not have to rent. I often use this with religious organizations, not-for-profits, and high schools. It is a great, low-cost way (if you don't have to rent a space to host the event) of bringing together local businesses and folks within the community. And guess what? You as the host get a chance to gather all of the contact information for every business and attendee. This is the ultimate inbound marketing campaign!

It does require much more work and coordination than other campaigns, but the relationships you will build as well as the contact data you will acquire is well worth the work.

Because each registered business is helping you to promote the event, you should see a pretty good turnout of attendees. Don't be afraid to charge if a registered business wants to upgrade by getting more space or using more electrical outlets than you are comfortable giving away for free.

Check with your insurance agent to make sure you are covered for all contingencies. It is a good idea to get special event coverage for the event. Find out the cost of the insurance coverage prior to announcing the event and you can change it from a free event to a low-cost event and have the participating businesses cover the cost of the special event insurance.

What can easily make this go from a low-cost, high-return event, to a high-cost event is the addition of food, drinks, and specialty items like entertainment, DJs, and other completely unnecessary extras. I have seen organizations screw up this type of campaign because they wanted to be impressive instead of efficient.

The more space you have available at no cost to you, the more electrical outlets you have available, and the more participating businesses you invite, the more effective this type of marketing campaign will be for your organization.

Campaign 21 – Drip Email Newsletter Campaign

Marketing Campaign: Drip Email Newsletter Campaign

Inbound Call-to-Action: Sign up for our newsletter

Inbound Call-to-Action Wording: Sign up for our information packed newsletter. Our easy to read, information-packed newsletter comes with our links to our latest videos, promotions, and discount coupons.

Marketing Tools: Data Super Center – Pre-written monthly newsletter templates, drip email functionality, merge field functionality, and contact management.

There are tons of email programs you can use for this type of campaign. The major 3 email tools we recommend that are not named the Data Super Center are www.mailchimp.com www.constantcontact.com and www.icontact.com.

Newsletters and drip email can have a great return on investment if you provide some value based information or at least some fun and entertaining information.

The Fun Facts E-Newsletter located in the Data Super Center is more focused on fun and entertaining information with some value information (such as referral request wording) sprinkled in the newsletter. This format is very effective and greatly increases the read rate of the e-newsletter.

Campaign 22 – Online Affiliates

<u>Marketing Campaign:</u> Use Online Affiliates to sell your products

<u>Inbound Call-to-Action:</u> Whatever wording and ads you and your affiliate agree on

<u>Inbound Call-to-Action Wording:</u> Whatever wording and ads you and your affiliate agree on

<u>Marketing Tools:</u> There are a lot of affiliate programs available to you. Here is a link that reviews the top affiliate programs: http://www.minterest.org/best-affiliate-programs-and-networks/.

An affiliate is a person or site that uses their online presence and contacts to market your products and services for a commission. If you have a product that has the ability to be promoted and sold by online affiliates, I strongly suggest you check it out. Not every product is a good candidate for affiliate marketing but those that are can do quite well.

Affiliate marketing is like having a sales team working for you 24 x 7. As with anything you have to make sure that there are quality controls in place to protect your brand, reputation, product, and money.

Make sure that you have the ability to quickly and permanently fire an affiliate if they are generating leads in a way that is deceptive or unethical. While it is easy to try and set up an internal tracking system for your affiliates, we suggest you go with an established affiliate program that you can afford. Some of the fees of the big boys and girls in the affiliate world are outrageous in my opinion, but with some research you can find the right program for you.

Be careful! There are a lot of shady affiliates on the internet. They will generate fake leads and charge you referral fees, they will register using the names of dead people, they will have their family and friends click on your links to drive up traffic, and every other trick our political system uses to make a candidate seem more popular. (Ha, Ha, Ha)

Paying a commission when an actual purchase occurs is the best way to make sure you are not getting ripped off by an affiliate.

Again, use this link to start your research on affiliate marketing: http://www.minterest.org/best-affiliate-programs-and-networks/.

Campaign 23 – Joint Presentation Meeting, Conference Call, or Webinar

Marketing Campaign: Joint Presentation Meeting, Conference Calls, and Webinars

Inbound Call-to-Action: Join our panel of experts

Inbound Call-to-Action Wording: Join our panel of experts as they explain how to ??? (Webinar topic). Our esteemed guest panel includes: 1. Name, title, area of expertise; 2. Name, title, area of expertise.

Marketing Tools: Data Super Center – Contact manager, email blast functionality, landing pages, and autoresponder functionality. There are many webinar tools available for your use. Here is a link that compares multiple tools: https://www.g2crowd.com/categories/web-conferencing/compare

Adding other presenters to your information meetings, conference calls, and webinars is a great way of getting more attendees as well as adding new perspectives and information.

Always look for joint presenters that bring a large network to the table. This expands both your network of potential prospects and your event attendees.

You can have your attendees register in advance, or, you can post the event information as part of your multi-channel marketing campaigns. From our experience, in general, conference calls work best when you supply the call information upfront, and webinars do best when an individual preregisters. I believe it is because a webinar means your attendees need to block off time in their day if they want to actually pay attention to the webinar, where a conference call still allows them to easily multi tasks.

Age of your target audience plays a role as well. A target audience of 55+ tends to do better with a conference call and prerecorded audio, while a younger target audience tends to do better with webinars and recorded video.

I mention conference calls, prerecorded audio, and videos because those types of campaigns can be used in place of a live joint presentation webinar.

Campaign 24 – Every Door Direct Postal Mail Campaign

Marketing Campaign: Every Door Direct Postal Mail Campaign

Inbound Call-to-Action: Use 3 different Calls-to-Actions on each mailing campaign

Inbound Call-to-Action Wording: Call us at 123-456-7890, Download our report by visiting www.mydomain/downloads, or listen to a short recorded message by calling 234-567-8901 that explains how we solve the problem of (trigger). This recording is available 24 x 7.

Marketing Tools: Data Super Center – Letter templates, inbound call tracking, recorded message functionality, and landing pages.

For the more traditional marketer a mailing campaign is a good way to generate inbound prospects.

The postal service has a program called Every Door Direct Mail that allows you to send a postal mail piece to every address on a postal route for a low cost. Here is the link: https://www.usps.com/business/every-door-direct-mail.htm. You can create your own mailings or use one of the recommended vendors on the Postal Service site.

We find that oversize postcards work best, followed by letters in oversized envelopes, and finally regularly sized letter envelopes.

Our recommended vendors for post cards are Postcard Mania and Vista Print, however if you have a local print shop or fulfillment house that can handle the design and printing of the post cards, use them, and still mail by using E.D.D.M.

Campaign 25 – Search Results Marketing including GPS Results

Marketing Campaign: Search Results Marketing including GPS Results

Inbound Call-to-Action: Based on the type of search the customer used to locate your information

Inbound Call-to-Action Wording: Based on the type of search the customer used to locate your information

Marketing Tools: All of the inbound functionality of the Data Super Center

Search results marketing is an integral part of SEO. There are tons of books available on SEO techniques, but I feel it is important that I bring up some key points specifically about Search Result Marketing. Here is a link to an excellent blog post on Search Results Marketing: http://www.wordstream.com/serp

1. Make sure that your business contact information is the same across the various search engines and local directories. Here is a link to the top 50 local directories – Top 50 Local Directories.

2. If you are not tech savvy, I strongly suggest that you use a SEO service. https://www.aabacosmallbusiness.com/local-listings (the former Yahoo! local directory) is a great service to use.

Register your business with GPS information services:

Along with internet searches, you want your business found on GPS device searches as well!

• If you want to be sure you've got a shot at inclusion on GPS device searches, you can report your business to the major mapping companies to make sure they have your information

• There are four primary GPS information providers:

NAVTEQ: mapreporter.navteq.com

Tele Atlas: mapfeedback.teleatlas.com

InfoUSA: dbupdate.infousa.com.

Google Maps: www.google.com/placesforbusiness

If you have a business with multiple locations or a chain of businesses, you might need to list each of them separately. In that case, both NAVTEQ and Tele Atlas have programs that will keep all of your locations up-to-date. You can check out NAVTEQ's Direct Access program and ContentLink program from Tele Atlas.

Garmin & TomTom, the leading GPS manufacturers in North America, license the maps and Points-of-Interest (POI) information in their GPS devices from two companies, NavTeq and TeleAtlas. Therefore, you must submit your business to both of these companies in order to be listed in the most popular GPS devices used by consumers.

Listing Your Business with NavTeq

1. Click here (https://mapreporter.navteq.com/?userType=CONSUMER&language=en#dashboard) to go to the NavTeq Map Reporter website,

2. Create a "Map Creator" account and log in,

3. Click on the "Find & Report" tab,

4. Search for your business name. If nothing is found, click on "Add a New Item to the Map" (Add your business exactly as you registered it with other search engines and directories),

5. Click on "Add a new POI,"

6. Fill out the form with your business' details,

7. Using the zoom function on the map, drag the map on the right until your business is approximately in the center of the map, then click "Mark Position on Map." A pink balloon will appear over the center of the map. You can fine tune the location of your listing by dragging the balloon directly over your business. When you are asked if this is the correct location, click on "Yes, Submit,"

8. Click "Next Step,"

9. Confirm the information is correct, then click "Send Report."

Listing Your Business with TeleAtlas

1. Click here (http://www.mapsharetool.com/external-iframe/external.jsp) to go to the TeleAtlas Map Feedback website,

2. I suggest you log in with your Google Log-On to help get your listing additional indexing support,

3. Under the Find Location button, type in your business' address,

4. Click "Find", and an arrow will appear at that address. If the location on the map is incorrect, you can drag the arrow to the correct location,

5. Under the "what to report" wording select "Point of Interest (POI),"

6. Select "Add a Point of Interest,"

7. Drag the "green pin" to the desired point of interest location,

8. Enter your business name and select a category. You may also add remarks to describe your business. Use the keywords and phrases that bring up your business in a Google search,

9. Click the "Submit" button,

10. Confirm the information is correct, then click "Submit Report."

*Please Note: This process only submits a request for your business to be added to the database. This request is subject to review by NavTeq & TeleAtlas. Also, your listing will not appear in existing GPS devices unless the system does an automatic update or the user updates the POI database on their device with the manufacturer. It could be a couple of months before you are consistently located using a GPS.

Campaign 26 – Email collection box on your website

Marketing Campaign: Email collection box on your website

Inbound Calls-to-Action: Sign up for our newsletter, download our report, give us your email address and receive a discount, receive our weekly specials by email, add yourself to our email list before you leave, etc.

Inbound Call-to-Action Wording: Based on the type of collection box you use on your website

Marketing Tools: All of the inbound functionality of the Data Super Center, along with a 3rd party collection box company.

While it might seem like a pain in the rear when you are on a website and an email collection box pops up, the reality is that you will build your email list 50% - 80% faster when you have an email collection box on your website or landing page.

At a minimum you should have a help tab that sits on each page of your site and an email collection box that pops up when a website visitor clicks to leave your site.

When it comes to website collection boxes with multiple functionality there is one company that stands head and shoulders above the competition (in my opinion) and that company is . . . Sumome.com: https://sumome.com/showcase.

93

They have a totally free service that is better than any paid service I have found. They also have premium services and tools that have much more functionality than I could ever explain in this short write-up.

Let me make it clear that I am not an affiliate, nor do I receive any type of compensation from sumome.com; they are just the best I have come across in this arena.

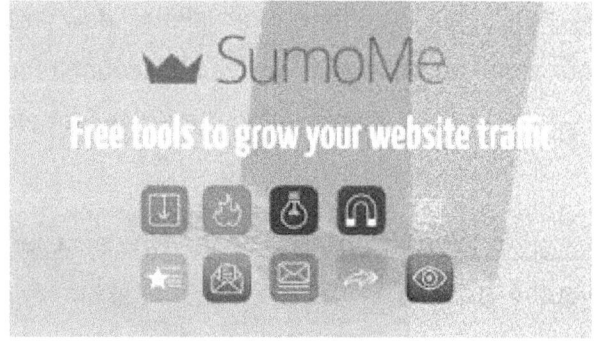

Final Thoughts

Just as the English language has over a million words built from 26 letters, I have given you the DNA to build 100s of inbound marketing campaigns simply by modifying the 26 campaigns I explained. You can change an online campaign into a postal mail campaign, or exchange video for audio, or exchange a call-in campaign for text-in campaign. The only thing limiting you is your creativity and the discipline to actually get a campaign up and running in your business.

It is not what you know, but what you do that makes your business successful. You must practice all 3 of the previously explained discipline types to make your business grow: Self-Discipline, Accountability, and Outsourcing. Be honest with yourself about what you will do and what you won't do. If you won't do it, and you won't hold someone else accountable for getting it done, but it needs to get done for your business to be successful, outsource it to an individual or company.

If you are an Insurance Agent anywhere in the world, and you can read English, Inspire a Nation Business Mentoring has the ultimate Insurance Agent Mentoring Program and Tools available for you. It is quick and easy to sign-up and you will have immediate access to the best, time-tested, low-cost processes, job-aids, scripts, video and audio training, and actual role-play conversations you can use to grow your agency.

One of the most powerful benefits of an Inspire a Nation Business Mentoring membership is the ability to schedule a monthly one-on-one call with an available business mentors who can help you understand where to go next in your business. Check it out at http://www.inspireanation.org/membershipinformation.

Our Insurance Agent version of the Data and Marketing Super Center will make the data management, tracking of inbound marketing campaigns, and automation of outbound marketing campaigns a snap.

Check it out at http://www.inspireanation.org/Data-Super-Center.

For the General Small Business we have:

The Data and Marketing Super Center – Non-Insurance Version. All of the same functionality, but fewer pre-built templates and workflows as the Insurance version since each industry and business model is unique.

The 10 Minute Business Mentoring Video Newsletter - We at Inspire a Nation Business Mentoring understand that it is difficult to stay up to date in today's marketing and business environment. That's why we created the "10 Minute Business Mentor Video Newsletter."

After you sign up for the newsletter, each month you will receive an email with a link to this video page.

The training videos will show you step by step how to implement one new marketing process in your business!

You no longer have to figure out what your next marketing campaign should be. We removed the guess work and give you the detailed, step-by-step, video training you need to get the campaign up and running in your business.

The cost? 10 minutes or less

Keep this book handy and please do the following as soon as you get a chance:

1. Write a review about the book on Amazon,

2. Send a copy as a gift to a friend, family member, or business contact that could use this information,

3. Add yourself to our monthly newsletter by texting your email address to 682-200-1808,

4. Get the latest updates, discount promotions, and information on upcoming mentoring and training events by downloading our mobile app - https://inspireanationmentoring.appsme.com.

Thanks again for reading this Book!

Billy R. Williams, PhD

President – Inspire a Nation Business Mentoring

www.inspireanation.org